Prayer Journal

&

Book of Remembrance

"And the LORD said unto Moses, Write this *for* a memorial in a book..."

Exodus 17:14

All scripture references are from the King James Bible.

Nathan Micaiah Noyes

FOREWORD

This prayer journal is filled with scriptures (all scripture is from the King James Bible). There are over 100 verses that will encourage you in prayer. It is designed for you to journal your prayer requests and also record when a prayer is answered and how it transpired. It is important to remember and praise God for answered prayer. This prayer journal is not something you need. You can pray anytime anywhere, but it will allow you to record and remember what God has done in answer to your prayers.

There are prayer lists followed by five pages of remembrance. It is recommended to use the list and pray until you receive an answer. Then, record it on the remembrance pages, which are the five pages that follow. Each page has a space for the date requested and the date answered.

Each prayer list is preceded by a special, self-explanatory page that will inspire you to pray for things that you may not have thought to pray for.

There is also an area for sermon notes and some special pages for praise. Knowing I do not pray enough, the intent of this book is to encourage prayer habits in myself and others.

The sermon notes section has 52 pages, one for each week of the year. Taking notes will allow you to reflect back on the Pastor's message.

There is a one year Bible reading plan. It is so important to read your Bible every day! I encourage you to read through your Bible as you journey through this prayer journal and book of remembrance.

At the end you will find a Christian allegory.

Select one scripture each week to meditate on and memorize. The verses listed were selected to build your faith, and encourage your prayer life.

PRAYER & BIBLE READING TREE

It takes roots to make fruit!

= Prayer

Leaf

= Answered Prayer

Fruit

= Bible Reading

Root

On the next page is your tree.
Each day you use this prayer journal
add a leaf to your tree. Each time
you read your daily Bible reading
add a root. Each time a prayer is
answered add a fruit.

"Jesus saith unto him, I am the way, the truth, and the life: no man cometh unto the Father, but by me."

John 14:6

YOUR TREE

Read your Bible and Pr

ROAD TO SALVATION

Romans 3:10,23,24 & 5:7,8 & 6:23 & 10:9-11

As it is written, There is none righteous, no, not one: For all have sinned, and come short of the glory of God; For when we were yet without strength, in due time Christ died for the ungodly. For scarcely for a righteous man will one die: yet peradventure for a good man some would even dare to die. But God commendeth his love toward us, in that, while we were yet sinners, Christ died for us. For the wages of sin is death; but the gift of God is eternal life through Jesus Christ our Lord. That if thou shalt confess with thy mouth the Lord Jesus, and shalt believe in thine heart that God hath raised him from the dead, thou shalt be saved. For with the heart man believeth unto righteousness; and with the mouth confession is made unto salvation. For the scripture saith, Whosoever believeth on him shall not be ashamed.

Admit you are a sinner and good works cannot save you. Repent, turn from sin to Jesus. He is the only One who can save you from sin and Hell. Tell others.

DECISION TIME

By: Pastor Frank Noyes

We need to ask ourselves four questions when we make a decision:

1. Have we prayed it through? (James 1:5-8)
2. Are we choosing the right way over the wrong way according to the Bible? (Ps.119:105, Prov. 1:10)
3. What is the spiritual thing to do or which choice will glorify Jesus the most? (Mk. 8:34-38, I Cor. 6:20)
4. Have we chosen the way of faith rather than the way of fear? (Is. 7:10-13)

Of course we need to consider all the information according to Luke 14:31-33 and Prov. 18:13. When possible we should always seek advice from spiritual people (I Kings 12:1-15, Prov. 12:15).

"Trust in the LORD with all thine heart; and lean not unto thine own understanding. In all thy ways acknowledge him, and he shall direct thy paths." Proverbs 3:5-6

"If I regard iniquity in my heart, the Lord will not hear *me:*"

Psalms 66:18

If we confess our sins, he is faithful and just to forgive us our sins, and to cleanse us from all unrighteousness.

I John 1:9

"If my people,
which are called by my name,
shall humble themselves,
and pray, and seek my face,
and turn from their wicked ways;
then will I hear from heaven,
and will forgive their sin,
and will heal their land."

II Chronicles 7:14

"After this manner therefore pray ye:
Our Father which art in heaven,
Hallowed be thy name.
Thy kingdom come.
Thy will be done in earth,
as *it is* in heaven.
Give us this day our daily bread.
And forgive us our debts,
as we forgive our debtors.
And lead us not into temptation,
but deliver us from evil:
For thine is the kingdom,
and the power, and the glory,
for ever. Amen."
Matthew 6:9-13

Paste a photo of
your family here.

PRAY FOR YOUR
FAMILY EVERY DAY!

PRAYER LIST

Date	Request
2-18	Dakota, Lauren + Charolette
218	Kaytlin, Isaac + Donald
218	Tina's trip (Safety)
218	New orders close to home?

"Now we know that God heareth not sinners: but if any man be a worshipper of God, and doeth his will, him he heareth."
John 9:31

PRAYER LIST

Date	Request

"Who in the days of his flesh, when he had offered up prayers and supplications with strong crying and tears unto him that was able to save him from death, and was heard in that he feared; Though he were a Son, yet learned he obedience by the things which he suffered; And being made perfect, he became the author of eternal salvation unto all them that obey him;"

Hebrews 5:7-9

PRAYER LIST

Date	Request

"O my God, incline thine ear, and hear; open thine eyes, and behold our desolations, and the city which is called by thy name: for we do not present our supplications before thee for our righteousnesses, but for thy great mercies."

Daniel 9:18

Date Requested

Write your request here:

Date Answered

Write your praise here:

"This poor man cried,
and the LORD heard *him,*
and saved him out of
all his troubles."

Psalms 34:6

Date Requested

Write your request here:

Date Answered

Write your praise here:

"Hearken unto the voice of my cry,
my King, and my God:
for unto thee will I pray."
Psalms 5:2

Date Requested

Write your request here:

Date Answered

Write your praise here:

"And this is the confidence that we have in him, that, if we ask any thing according to his will, he heareth us: And if we know that he hear us, whatsoever we ask, we know that we have the petitions that we desired of him."

I John 5:14-15

Date Requested

Write your request here:

Date Answered

Write your praise here:

"I will cry unto God most high; unto God that performeth *all things* for me."
Psalms 57:2

Date Requested

Write your request here:

Date Answered

Write your praise here:

"...ye have not, because ye ask not. Ye ask, and receive not, because ye ask amiss, that ye may consume *it* upon your lusts."
James 4:2-3

Cell Phone Challenge

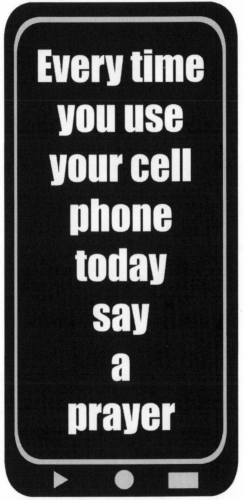

Every time you use your cell phone today say a prayer

I use my cell phone too much, but I do not pray enough.

"The LORD *is* far from the wicked: but he heareth the prayer of the righteous."

Psalms 15:29

PRAYER LIST

Date	Request

"Is any among you afflicted?
let him pray..."
James 5:13

PRAYER LIST

Date	Request

"Now therefore, O our God, hear the prayer of thy servant, and his supplications, and cause thy face to shine upon thy sanctuary that is desolate, for the Lord's sake."

Daniel 9:17

PRAYER LIST

Date	Request

"They shall come with weeping, and with supplications will I lead them: I will cause them to walk by the rivers of waters in a straight way, wherein they shall not stumble: for I am a father to Israel, and Ephraim *is* my firstborn."

Jeremiah 31:9

Date Requested

Write your request here:

Date Answered

Write your praise here:

"Confess *your* faults one to another,
and pray one for another,
that ye may be healed. The effectual
fervent prayer of a righteous man
availeth much. Elias was a man subject
to like passions as we are, and he
prayed earnestly that it might not rain:
and it rained not on the earth by the
space of three years and six months.
And he prayed again, and the heaven
gave rain, and the earth brought forth
her fruit."
James 5:16-18

Date Requested

Write your request here:

Date Answered

Write your praise here:

"For verily I say unto you, That whosoever shall say unto this mountain, Be thou removed, and be thou cast into the sea; and shall not doubt in his heart, but shall believe that those things which he saith shall come to pass; he shall have whatsoever he saith."

Mark 11:23

Date Requested

Write your request here:

Date Answered

Write your praise here:

"Therefore I say unto you, What things soever ye desire, when ye pray, believe that ye receive *them,* and ye shall have *them.*

Mark 11:24

Date Requested

Write your request here:

Date Answered

Write your praise here:

"And when ye stand praying, forgive, if ye have ought against any: that your Father also which is in heaven may forgive you your trespasses. But if ye do not forgive, neither will your Father which is in heaven forgive your trespasses."
Mark 11:25-26

Date Requested

Write your request here:

Date Answered

Write your praise here:

"As far as the east is from the west, *so* far hath he removed our transgressions from us."

Psalms 103:12

Make a list of all your SINS

_____

_____

_____

_____

_____

_____

_____

_____

_____

Make things right with those you have wronged. Pray, confess these sins to God. Then burn this list.

PRAYER LIST

Date	Request

"Yet have thou respect unto the prayer of thy servant, and to his supplication, O LORD my God, to hearken unto the cry and to the prayer, which thy servant prayeth before thee to day:"
I Kings 8:28

PRAYER LIST

Date	Request

"A voice was heard upon the high places, weeping *and* supplications of the children of Israel: for they have perverted their way, *and* they have forgotten the LORD their God."

Jeremiah 3:21

PRAYER LIST

Date	Request

"Hear my prayer, O LORD, give ear to my supplications: in thy faithfulness answer me, *and* in thy righteousness."

Psalms 143:1

Date Requested

Write your request here:

Date Answered

Write your praise here:

"Hear me when I call, O God of my righteousness: thou hast enlarged me *when I was* in distress; have mercy upon me, and hear my prayer."

Psalms 4:1

Date Requested

Write your request here:

Date Answered

Write your praise here:

"My voice shalt thou hear in the morning, O LORD; in the morning will I direct *my prayer* unto thee, and will look up."

Psalms 5:3

Date Requested

Write your request here:

Date Answered

Write your praise here:

"The LORD hath heard my supplication;
the LORD will receive my prayer."

Psalms 6:9

Date Requested

Write your request here:

Date Answered

Write your praise here:

"Hear the right, O LORD, attend unto my cry, give ear unto my prayer, *that goeth* not out of feigned lips."

Psalms 17:1

Date Requested

Write your request here:

Date Answered

Write your praise here:

"And when thou prayest, thou shalt not be as the hypocrites *are:* for they love to pray standing in the synagogues and in the corners of the streets, that they may be seen of men. Verily I say unto you, They have their reward. But thou, when thou prayest, enter into thy closet, and when thou hast shut thy door, pray to thy Father which is in secret; and thy Father which seeth in secret shall reward thee openly."

Matthew 6:5-6

Pray for our President!

"But I say unto you, Love your enemies, bless them that curse you, do good to them that hate you, and pray for them which despitefully use you, and persecute you;"

Matthew 5:44

PRAYER LIST

Date	Request

"Hear my prayer, O God; give ear to the words of my mouth."

Psalms 54:2

PRAYER LIST

Date	Request

"I said unto the LORD, Thou *art* my God: hear the voice of my supplications, O LORD."

Psalms 140:6

PRAYER LIST

Date	Request

"Lord, hear my voice: let thine ears be attentive to the voice of my supplications."

Psalms 130:2

Date Requested

Write your request here:

Date Answered

Write your praise here:

"But when ye pray, use not vain repetitions, as the heathen *do:* for they think that they shall be heard for their much speaking. Be not ye therefore like unto them: for your Father knoweth what things ye have need of, before ye ask him."

Matthew 6:7-8

Date Requested

Write your request here:

Date Answered

Write your praise here:

"Watch and pray, that ye enter not into temptation: the spirit indeed *is* willing, but the flesh *is* weak."
Matthew 26:41

Date Requested

Write your request here:

Date Answered

Write your praise here:

"Be careful for nothing; but in every thing by prayer and supplication with thanksgiving let your requests be made known unto God."

Philippians 4:6

Date Requested

Write your request here:

Date Answered

Write your praise here:

"Praying always with all prayer and supplication in the Spirit, and watching thereunto with all perseverance and supplication for all saints;"

Ephesians 6:18

Date Requested

Write your request here:

Date Answered

Write your praise here:

"I will greatly praise the LORD with my mouth; yea, I will praise him among the multitude."

Psalms 109:30

PRAISE GOD

Use this page to praise God
for what he has done!

"But ye, beloved, building up yourselves on your most holy faith, praying in the Holy Ghost, Keep yourselves in the love of God, looking for the mercy of our Lord Jesus Christ unto eternal life."

Jude 1:20-21

PRAYER LIST

Date	Request

"I cried unto the LORD with my voice; with my voice unto the LORD did I make my supplication."

Psalms 142:1

PRAYER LIST

Date	Request

"I love the LORD, because he hath heard my voice *and* my supplications."

Psalms 116:1

PRAYER LIST

Date	Request

"Give ear, O LORD, unto my prayer; and attend to the voice of my supplications."

Psalms 86:6

Date Requested

Write your request here:

Date Answered

Write your praise here:

"Hear me, O LORD, hear me, that this people may know that thou *art* the LORD God, and *that* thou hast turned their heart back again."

I Kings 18:37

Date Requested

Write your request here:

Date Answered

Write your praise here:

"Oh that one would hear me! behold, my desire *is, that* the Almighty would answer me, and *that* mine adversary had written a book."

Job 31:35

Date Requested

Write your request here:

Date Answered

Write your praise here:

"I have called upon thee, for thou wilt hear me, O God: incline thine ear unto me, *and* hear my speech."

Psalms 17:6

Date Requested

Write your request here:

Date Answered

Write your praise here:

"Therefore I will look unto the LORD; I will wait for the God of my salvation: my God will hear me."

Micah 7:7

Date Requested

Write your request here:

Date Answered

Write your praise here:

"Every man praying or prophesying, having *his* head covered, dishonoureth his head."

I Corinthians 11:4

Pray for Missionaries!

Paste a photo of a missionary

"And how shall they preach, except they be sent? as it is written, How beautiful are the feet of them that preach the gospel of peace, and bring glad tidings of good things!"

Romans 10:15

"And whiles I *was* speaking, and praying, and confessing my sin and the sin of my people Israel, and presenting my supplication before the LORD my God for the holy mountain of my God; Yea, whiles I *was* speaking in prayer, even the man Gabriel, whom I had seen in the vision at the beginning, being caused to fly swiftly, touched me about the time of the evening oblation. And he informed *me,* and talked with me, and said, O Daniel, I am now come forth to give thee skill and understanding. At the beginning of thy supplications the commandment came forth, and I am come to shew *thee;* for thou *art* greatly beloved: therefore understand the matter, and consider the vision."

Daniel 9:20-23

PRAYER LIST

Date	Request

"We give thanks to God and the Father of our Lord Jesus Christ, praying always for you, Since we heard of your faith in Christ Jesus, and of the love *which ye have* to all the saints, For the hope which is laid up for you in heaven, whereof ye heard before in the word of the truth of the gospel;"

Colossians 1:3-5

PRAYER LIST

Date	Request

"For I said in my haste, I am cut off from before thine eyes: nevertheless thou heardest the voice of my supplications when I cried unto thee."

Psalms 31:22

PRAYER LIST

Date	Request

"Blessed *be* the LORD, because he hath heard the voice of my supplications."

Psalms 28:6

Date Requested

Write your request here:

Date Answered

Write your praise here:

"But every woman that prayeth or prophesieth with *her* head uncovered dishonoureth her head: for that is even all one as if she were shaven. For if the woman be not covered, let her also be shorn: but if it be a shame for a woman to be shorn or shaven, let her be covered."

I Corinthians 11:5-6

Date Requested

Write your request here:

Date Answered

Write your praise here:

"Rejoicing in hope; patient in tribulation; continuing instant in prayer;"
Romans 12:12

Date Requested

Write your request here:

Date Answered

Write your praise here:

"If ye then, being evil, know how to give good gifts unto your children, how much more shall your Father which is in heaven give good things to them that ask him?"
Matthew 7:11

Date Requested

Write your request here:

Date Answered

Write your praise here:

"And it came to pass in those days, that he went out into a mountain to pray, and continued all night in prayer to God."

Luke 6:12

Date Requested

Write your request here:

Date Answered

Write your praise here:

"For if our heart condemn us, God is greater than our heart, and knoweth all things. Beloved, if our heart condemn us not, *then* have we confidence toward God. And whatsoever we ask, we receive of him, because we keep his commandments, and do those things that are pleasing in his sight."
I John 3:20-22

Spend 3 minutes

thinking about how far God has brought you.

Therefore if any man be in Christ, he is a new creature: old things are passed away; behold, all things are become new.

II Corinthians 5:17

"Return to thine own house, and shew how great things God hath done unto thee. And he went his way, and published throughout the whole city how great things Jesus had done unto him."

Luke 8:39

PRAYER LIST

Date	Request

"Jesus answered and said unto her, If thou knewest the gift of God, and who it is that saith to thee, Give me to drink; thou wouldest have asked of him, and he would have given thee living water."

John 4:10

PRAYER LIST

Date	Request

"Hear the voice of my supplications, when I cry unto thee, when I lift up my hands toward thy holy oracle."

Psalms 28:2

PRAYER LIST

Date	Request

"If they return to thee with all their heart and with all their soul in the land of their captivity, whither they have carried them captives, and pray toward their land, which thou gavest unto their fathers, and *toward* the city which thou hast chosen, and toward the house which I have built for thy name: Then hear thou from the heavens, *even* from thy dwelling place, their prayer and their supplications, and maintain their cause, and forgive thy people which have sinned against thee."
II Chronicles 6:38-39

Date Requested

Write your request here:

Date Answered

Write your praise here:

"And he spake a parable unto them *to this end,* that men ought always to pray, and not to faint;"

Luke 18:1

Date Requested

Write your request here:

Date Answered

Write your praise here:

"Likewise the Spirit also helpeth our infirmities: for we know not what we should pray for as we ought: but the Spirit itself maketh intercession for us with groanings which cannot be uttered. And he that searcheth the hearts knoweth what *is* the mind of the Spirit, because he maketh intercession for the saints according to *the will of* God. And we know that all things work together for good to them that love God, to them who are the called according to *his* purpose."
Romans 8:26-28

Date Requested

Write your request here:

Date Answered

Write your praise here:

"For I know the thoughts that I think toward you, saith the LORD, thoughts of peace, and not of evil, to give you an expected end. Then shall ye call upon me, and ye shall go and pray unto me, and I will hearken unto you. And ye shall seek me, and find *me,* when ye shall search for me with all your heart."
Jeremiah 29:11-13

Date Requested

Write your request here:

Date Answered

Write your praise here:

"Saying, There was in a city a judge, which feared not God, neither regarded man: And there was a widow in that city; and she came unto him, saying, Avenge me of mine adversary. And he would not for a while: but afterward he said within himself, Though I fear not God, nor regard man; Yet because this widow troubleth me, I will avenge her, lest by her continual coming she weary me. And the Lord said, Hear what the unjust judge saith. And shall not God avenge his own elect, which cry day and night unto him, though he bear long with them?"
Luke 18:2-7

Date Requested

Write your request here:

Date Answered

Write your praise here:

"I exhort therefore, that, first of all, supplications, prayers, intercessions, *and* giving of thanks, be made for all men; For kings, and *for* all that are in authority; that we may lead a quiet and peaceable life in all godliness and honesty. For this *is* good and acceptable in the sight of God our Saviour;"

I Timothy 2:1-3

Pray for those in authority.

Write out your prayer below.

"Continue in prayer, and watch in the same with thanksgiving;"
Colossians 4:2

PRAYER LIST

Date	Request

"Pray without ceasing."
I Thessalonians 5:17

PRAYER LIST

Date	Request

"Heal me, O LORD, and I shall be healed; save me, and I shall be saved: for thou *art* my praise."

Jeremiah 17:14

PRAYER LIST

Date	Request

"I said, LORD, be merciful unto me: heal my soul; for I have sinned against thee."

Psalms 41:4

Date Requested

Write your request here:

Date Answered

Write your praise here:

"I will therefore that men pray every where, lifting up holy hands, without wrath and doubting."
I Timothy 2:8

Date Requested

Write your request here:

Date Answered

Write your praise here:

"What shall we then say to these things? If God *be* for us, who *can be* against us? He that spared not his own Son, but delivered him up for us all, how shall he not with him also freely give us all things?"

Romans 8:31-32

Date Requested

Write your request here:

Date Answered

Write your praise here:

"If any of you lack wisdom, let him ask of God, that giveth to all *men* liberally, and upbraideth not; and it shall be given him. But let him ask in faith, nothing wavering. For he that wavereth is like a wave of the sea driven with the wind and tossed. For let not that man think that he shall receive any thing of the Lord."

James 1:5-7

Date Requested

Write your request here:

Date Answered

Write your praise here:

"Verily I say unto you, Whatsoever ye shall bind on earth shall be bound in heaven: and whatsoever ye shall loose on earth shall be loosed in heaven. Again I say unto you, That if two of you shall agree on earth as touching any thing that they shall ask, it shall be done for them of my Father which is in heaven. For where two or three are gathered together in my name, there am I in the midst of them."
Matthew 18:18-20

Date Requested

Write your request here:

Date Answered

Write your praise here:

"But I say unto you which hear, Love your enemies, do good to them which hate you, Bless them that curse you, and pray for them which despitefully use you."

Luke 6:27-28

Make a list of people you do not like.

_____

_____

_____

_____

_____

_____

_____

_____

Pray for them!

"The sacrifice of the wicked *is* an abomination to the LORD: but the prayer of the upright *is* his delight."

Proverbs 15:8

PRAYER LIST

Date	Request

"Watch ye therefore, and pray always, that ye may be accounted worthy to escape all these things that shall come to pass, and to stand before the Son of man."

Luke 21:36

PRAYER LIST

Date	Request

"Have mercy upon me, O LORD; for I *am* weak: O LORD, heal me; for my bones are vexed."

Psalms 6:2

PRAYER LIST

Date	Request

"And straightway the father of the child cried out, and said with tears, Lord, I believe; help thou mine unbelief."

Mark 9:24

Date Requested

Write your request here:

Date Answered

Write your praise here:

"Finally, brethren, pray for us, that the word of the Lord may have *free* course, and be glorified, even as *it is* with you:"

II Thessalonians 3:1

Date Requested

Write your request here:

Date Answered

Write your praise here:

"For this cause we also, since the day we heard *it,* do not cease to pray for you, and to desire that ye might be filled with the knowledge of his will in all wisdom and spiritual understanding; That ye might walk worthy of the Lord unto all pleasing, being fruitful in every good work, and increasing in the knowledge of God; Strengthened with all might, according to his glorious power, unto all patience and longsuffering with joyfulness; Giving thanks unto the Father, which hath made us meet to be partakers of the inheritance of the saints in light: Who hath delivered us from the power of darkness, and hath translated *us* into the kingdom of his dear Son: In whom we have redemption through his blood, *even* the forgiveness of sins:"
Colossians 1:9-14

Date Requested

Write your request here:

Date Answered

Write your praise here:

"Brethren, pray for us."

I Thessalonians 5:25

Date Requested

Write your request here:

Date Answered

Write your praise here:

"Moreover as for me, God forbid that I should sin against the LORD in ceasing to pray for you: but I will teach you the good and the right way:"

I Samuel 12:23

Date Requested

Write your request here:

Date Answered

Write your praise here:

"Pray for the peace of Jerusalem: they shall prosper that love thee. Peace be within thy walls, *and* prosperity within thy palaces."
Psalms 122:6-7

Pray for the peace of Jerusalem!

Write out your prayer above.

"For *there is* one God, and one mediator between God and men, the man Christ Jesus;"

I Timothy 2:5

PRAYER LIST

Date	Request

"For what nation *is there so* great, who *hath* God *so* nigh unto them, as the LORD our God *is* in all *things that* we call upon him *for?*"

Deuteronomy 4:7

PRAYER LIST

Date	Request

"And the Lord said, If ye had faith as a grain of mustard seed, ye might say unto this sycamine tree, Be thou plucked up by the root, and be thou planted in the sea; and it should obey you."

Luke 17:6

PRAYER LIST

Date	Request

"And there came a leper to him, beseeching him, and kneeling down to him, and saying unto him, If thou wilt, thou canst make me clean. And Jesus, moved with compassion, put forth *his* hand, and touched him, and saith unto him, I will; be thou clean."

Mark 1:40-41

Date Requested

Write your request here:

Date Answered

Write your praise here:

"For God is my witness, whom I serve
with my spirit in the gospel of his Son,
that without ceasing I make mention of
you always in my prayers;"

Romans 1:9

Date Requested

Write your request here:

Date Answered

Write your praise here:

"I will call upon the LORD, *who is worthy* to be praised: so shall I be saved from mine enemies."

Psalms 18:3

Date Requested

Write your request here:

Date Answered

Write your praise here:

"Give thanks unto the LORD, call upon his name, make known his deeds among the people."

I Chronicles 16:8

Date Requested

Write your request here:

Date Answered

Write your praise here:

"As for me, I will call upon God; and the LORD shall save me."

Psalms 55:16

Date Requested

Write your request here:

Date Answered

Write your praise here:

"Obey them that have the rule over you, and submit yourselves: for they watch for your souls, as they that must give account, that they may do it with joy, and not with grief: for that *is* unprofitable for you. Pray for us: for we trust we have a good conscience, in all things willing to live honestly."
Hebrews 13:17-18

Pray for your pastor!

Paste a photo of
your
pastor here.

Pray for your pastor!

"Unto the church of God which is at Corinth, to them that are sanctified in Christ Jesus, called *to be* saints, with all that in every place call upon the name of Jesus Christ our Lord, both theirs and ours: Grace *be* unto you, and peace, from God our Father, and *from* the Lord Jesus Christ."

I Corinthians 1:2-3

PRAYER LIST

Date	Request

"And he cometh, and findeth them sleeping, and saith unto Peter, Simon, sleepest thou? couldest not thou watch one hour? Watch ye and pray, lest ye enter into temptation. The spirit truly *is* ready, but the flesh *is* weak."

Mark 14:37-38

PRAYER LIST

Date	Request

"And it came to pass, when he was in a certain city, behold a man full of leprosy: who seeing Jesus fell on *his* face, and besought him, saying, Lord, if thou wilt, thou canst make me clean. And he put forth *his* hand, and touched him, saying, I will: be thou clean. And immediately the leprosy departed from him."

Luke 5:12-13

PRAYER LIST

Date	Request

"And, behold, a woman, which was diseased with an issue of blood twelve years, came behind *him,* and touched the hem of his garment: For she said within herself, If I may but touch his garment, I shall be whole. But Jesus turned him about, and when he saw her, he said, Daughter, be of good comfort; thy faith hath made thee whole. And the woman was made whole from that hour."

Matthew 9:20-22

Date Requested

Write your request here:

Date Answered

Write your praise here:

"Take ye heed, watch and pray: for ye know not when the time is."

Mark 13:33

Date Requested

Write your request here:

Date Answered

Write your praise here:

"For the scripture saith, Whosoever believeth on him shall not be ashamed. For there is no difference between the Jew and the Greek: for the same Lord over all is rich unto all that call upon him. For whosoever shall call upon the name of the Lord shall be saved."
Romans 10:11-13

Date Requested

Write your request here:

Date Answered

Write your praise here:

"Because he hath inclined his ear unto me, therefore will I call upon *him* as long as I live."

Psalms 116:2

Date Requested

Write your request here:

Date Answered

Write your praise here:

"In the day of my trouble I will call upon thee: for thou wilt answer me."

Psalms 86:7

Date Requested

Write your request here:

Date Answered

Write your praise here:

"Then saith he unto his disciples, The harvest truly *is* plenteous, but the labourers *are* few; Pray ye therefore the Lord of the harvest, that he will send forth labourers into his harvest."

Matthew 9:37-38

Pray for God to send labourers into his field!

Write your prayer out above.

"Give ear to my words, O LORD, consider my meditation."

Psalms 5:1

PRAYER LIST

Date	Request

"Hear my prayer, O LORD, and give ear unto my cry; hold not thy peace at my tears: for I *am* a stranger with thee, *and* a sojourner, as all my fathers *were*."

Psalms 39:12

PRAYER LIST

Date	Request

"And a woman having an issue of blood twelve years, which had spent all her living upon physicians, neither could be healed of any,   Came behind *him,* and touched the border of his garment: and immediately her issue of blood stanched.   And Jesus said, Who touched me? When all denied, Peter and they that were with him said, Master, the multitude throng thee and press *thee,* and sayest thou, Who touched me?   And Jesus said, Somebody hath touched me: for I perceive that virtue is gone out of me. And when the woman saw that she was not hid, she came trembling, and falling down before him, she declared unto him before all the people for what cause she had touched him, and how she was healed immediately.   And he said unto her, Daughter, be of good comfort: thy faith hath made thee whole; go in peace."
Luke 8:43-48

PRAYER LIST

Date	Request

"And as he entered into a certain village, there met him ten men that were lepers, which stood afar off: And they lifted up *their* voices, and said, Jesus, Master, have mercy on us. And when he saw *them,* he said unto them, Go shew yourselves unto the priests. And it came to pass, that, as they went, they were cleansed. And one of them, when he saw that he was healed, turned back, and with a loud voice glorified God, And fell down on *his* face at his feet, giving him thanks: and he was a Samaritan. And Jesus answering said, Were there not ten cleansed? but where *are* the nine? There are not found that returned to give glory to God, save this stranger. And he said unto him, Arise, go thy way: thy faith hath made thee whole."

Luke 17:12-19

Date Requested

Write your request here:

Date Answered

Write your praise here:

"Now when Daniel knew that the writing was signed, he went into his house; and his windows being open in his chamber toward Jerusalem, he kneeled upon his knees three times a day, and prayed, and gave thanks before his God, as he did aforetime."

Daniel 6:10

Date Requested

Write your request here:

Date Answered

Write your praise here:

"And when Peter was come to himself, he said, Now I know of a surety, that the Lord hath sent his angel, and hath delivered me out of the hand of Herod, and *from* all the expectation of the people of the Jews. And when he had considered *the thing,* he came to the house of Mary the mother of John, whose surname was Mark; where many were gathered together praying."

Acts 12:11-12

Date Requested

Write your request here:

Date Answered

Write your praise here:

"For what thanks can we render to God again for you, for all the joy wherewith we joy for your sakes before our God; Night and day praying exceedingly that we might see your face, and might perfect that which is lacking in your faith?"

I Thessalonians 3:9-10

Date Requested

Write your request here:

Date Answered

Write your praise here:

"And they continued stedfastly in the apostles' doctrine and fellowship, and in breaking of bread, and in prayers."

Acts 2:42

Date Requested

Write your request here:

Date Answered

Write your praise here:

"And when he looked on him, he was afraid, and said, What is it, Lord? And he said unto him, Thy prayers and thine alms are come up for a memorial before God."

Acts 10:4

Make a list of your coworkers or classmates.

Pray for them daily.

_____

_____

_____

_____

_____

_____

_____

_____

_____

_____

_____

_____

_____

_____

"For ye have not received the spirit of bondage again to fear; but ye have received the Spirit of adoption, whereby we cry, Abba, Father."

Romans 8:15

PRAYER LIST

Date	Request

"And, behold, there came a leper and worshipped him, saying, Lord, if thou wilt, thou canst make me clean. And Jesus put forth *his* hand, and touched him, saying, I will; be thou clean. And immediately his leprosy was cleansed."
Matthew 8:2-3

PRAYER LIST

Date	Request

"Bow down thine ear to me; deliver me speedily: be thou my strong rock, for an house of defence to save me."

Psalms 31:2

PRAYER LIST

Date	Request

"Likewise, ye husbands, dwell with *them* according to knowledge, giving honour unto the wife, as unto the weaker vessel, and as being heirs together of the grace of life; that your prayers be not hindered."

I Peter 3:7

"These words spake Jesus, and lifted up his eyes to heaven, and said, Father, the hour is come; glorify thy Son, that thy Son also may glorify thee: As thou hast given him power over all flesh, that he should give eternal life to as many as thou hast given him. And this is life eternal, that they might know thee the only true God, and Jesus Christ, whom thou hast sent. I have glorified thee on the earth: I have finished the work which thou gavest me to do. And now, O Father, glorify thou me with thine own self with the glory which I had with thee before the world was. I have manifested thy name unto the men which thou gavest me out of the world: thine they were, and thou gavest them me; and they have kept thy word. Now they have known that all things whatsoever thou hast given me are of thee. For I have given unto them the words which thou gavest me; and they have received *them,* and have known surely that I came out from thee, and they have believed that thou didst send me. I pray for them: I pray not for the world, but for them which thou hast given me; for they are thine. And all mine are thine, and thine are mine; and I am glorified in them. And now I am no more in the world, but these are in the world, and I come to thee. Holy Father, keep through thine own name those whom thou hast given me, that they may be one, as we *are.* While I was with them in the world, I kept them in thy name: those that thou gavest me I have kept, and none of them is lost, but the son of perdition; that the scripture might be fulfilled. And now come I to thee; and these things I speak in the world, that they might have my joy fulfilled in themselves. I have given them thy word; and the world hath hated them, because they are not of the world, even as I am not of the world. I pray not that thou shouldest take them out of the world, but that thou shouldest keep them from the evil. They are not of the world, even as I am not of the world. Sanctify them through thy truth: thy word is truth. As thou hast sent me into the world, even so have I also sent them into the world. And for their sakes I sanctify myself, that they also might be sanctified through the truth. Neither pray I for these alone, but for them also which shall believe on me through their word; That they all may be one; as thou, Father, *art* in me, and I in thee, that they also may be one in us: that the world may believe that thou hast sent me. And the glory which thou gavest me I have given them; that they may be one, even as we are one: I in them, and thou in me, that they may be made perfect in one; and that the world may know that thou hast sent me, and hast loved them, as thou hast loved me. Father, I will that they also, whom thou hast given me, be with me where I am; that they may behold my glory, which thou hast given me: for thou lovedst me before the foundation of the world. O righteous Father, the world hath not known thee: but I have known thee, and these have known that thou hast sent me. And I have declared unto them thy name, and will declare *it:* that the love wherewith thou hast loved me may be in them, and I in them."

John 17:1-26

FAST AND PRAY TODAY

Spend the day fasting and praying.

Moreover when ye fast, be not, as the hypocrites, of a sad countenance: for they disfigure their faces, that they may appear unto men to fast. Verily I say unto you, They have their reward. But thou, when thou fastest, anoint thine head, and wash thy face; That thou appear not unto men to fast, but unto thy Father which is in secret: and thy Father, which seeth in secret, shall reward thee openly.

Matthew 6:16-18

Date of fast:_____

"But be ye doers of the word, and not hearers only, deceiving your own selves."

James 1:22

The smallest deed that I have done is greater than the greatest deed I have ever thought to do, and left undone.

Nathan M. Noyes

Sermon Notes

Title: _____ Date:_____

Sermon Notes

Title: _____ Date:_____

Sermon Notes

Title: _____ Date: _____

Sermon Notes

Title: _____   Date: _____

Sermon Notes

Title: _____ Date: _____

Sermon Notes

Title: _____ Date:_____

Sermon Notes

Title: _____   Date: _____

Sermon Notes

Title: _____ Date: _____

Sermon Notes

Title: _____ Date:_____

Sermon Notes

Title: _____ Date:_____

Sermon Notes

Title: _____ Date: _____

Sermon Notes

Title: _____ Date: _____

Sermon Notes

Title: _____ Date:_____

Sermon Notes

Title: _____ Date: _____

Sermon Notes

Title: _____ Date: _____

Sermon Notes

Title: _____ Date:_____

Sermon Notes

Title: _____ Date: _____

Sermon Notes

Title: _____ Date: _____

Sermon Notes

Title: _____ Date:_____

Sermon Notes

Title: _____ Date: _____

Sermon Notes

Title: _____ Date: _____

Sermon Notes

Title: _____ Date:_____

Sermon Notes

Title: _____ Date:_____

Sermon Notes

Title: _____ Date:_____

Sermon Notes

Title: _____ Date: _____

Sermon Notes

Title: _____ Date: _____

Sermon Notes

Title: _____ Date:_____

Sermon Notes

Title: _____ Date: _____

Sermon Notes

Title: _____ Date:_____

Sermon Notes

Title: _____ Date: _____

Sermon Notes

Title: _____ Date: _____

Sermon Notes

Title: _____ Date: _____

Sermon Notes

Title: _____ Date: _____

Sermon Notes

Title: _____ Date:_____

Sermon Notes

Title: _____   Date: _____

Sermon Notes

Title: _____ Date: _____

Sermon Notes

Title: _____ Date: _____

Sermon Notes

Title: _____ Date:_____

Sermon Notes

Title: _____ Date: _____

Sermon Notes

Title: _____ Date:_____

Sermon Notes

Title: _____ Date: _____

Sermon Notes

Title: _____ Date: _____

Sermon Notes

Title: _____ Date: _____

Sermon Notes

Title: _____ Date: _____

Sermon Notes

Title: _____   Date: _____

Sermon Notes

Title: _____ Date: _____

Sermon Notes

Title: _____ Date: _____

Sermon Notes

Title: _____   Date:_____

Sermon Notes

Title: _____ Date: _____

Sermon Notes

Title: _____ Date: _____

Sermon Notes

Title: _____ Date: _____

Sermon Notes

Title: _____ Date: _____

"And that from a child thou hast known the holy scriptures, which are able to make thee wise unto salvation through faith which is in Christ Jesus.
All scripture *is* given by inspiration of God, and *is* profitable for doctrine, for reproof, for correction, for instruction in righteousness:
That the man of God may be perfect, throughly furnished unto all good works."
II Timothy 3:15-17

YEAR BIBLE READING PLAN

Each day read the chapters listed. After you read the daily reading put a line through it.
Example: ~~Gen. 1-4~~

Gen. 1-4			Judg. 7-8
Gen. 5-8	Ex. 31-33	Num. 28-30	Judg. 9-10
Gen. 9-12	Ex. 34-36	Num. 31-32	Judg. 11-14
Gen. 13-16	Ex. 37-38	Num. 33-36	Judg. 15-17
Gen. 17-19	Ex. 39-40	Deut. 1-2	Judg. 18-19
Gen. 20-23	Lev. 1-4	Deut. 3-4	Judg. 20-21
Gen. 24-25	Lev. 5-7	Deut. 5-7	Ruth 1-4
Gen. 26-27	Lev. 8-9	Deut. 8-10	I Sam. 1-3
Gen. 28-30	Lev. 10-12	Deut. 11-13	I Sam. 4-8
Gen. 31-32	Lev. 13-14	Deut. 14-16	I Sam. 9-11
Gen. 33-36	Lev. 15-16	Deut. 17-20	I Sam. 12-13
Gen. 37-39	Lev. 17-20	Deut. 21-23	I Sam. 14-16
Gen. 40-41	Lev. 21-22	Deut. 24-27	I Sam. 17-18
Gen. 42-44	Lev. 23-25	Deut. 28-29	I Sam. 19-21
Gen. 45-47	Lev. 26-27	Deut. 30-31	I Sam. 22-24
Gen. 48-50	Num. 1-2	Deut. 32-34	I Sam. 25-27
Ex. 1-3	Num. 3-4	Josh. 1-4	I Sam. 28-31
Ex. 4-7	Num. 5-6	Josh. 5-7	II Sam. 1-2
Ex. 8-9	Num. 7-8	Josh. 8-9	II Sam. 3-6
Ex. 10-12	Num. 9-11	Josh. 10-12	II Sam. 7-10
Ex. 13-15	Num. 12-14	Josh. 13-16	II Sam. 11-12
Ex. 16-18	Num. 15-16	Josh. 17-18	II Sam. 13-15
Ex. 19-22	Num. 17-19	Josh. 19-21	II Sam. 16-17
Ex. 23-25	Num. 20-21	Josh. 22-24	II Sam. 18-19
Ex. 26-28	Num. 22-25	Judg. 1-3	II Sam. 20-22
Ex. 29-30	Num. 26-27	Judg. 4-6	II Sam. 23-24

"Thy word *is* a lamp unto my feet, and a light unto my path."
Psalms 119:105

YEAR BIBLE READING PLAN

Each day read the chapters listed. After you read the daily reading put a line through it.

Example: ~~Gen. 1-4~~

I Kings 1-2			Ps. 104-107
I Kings 3-5	I Chr. 19-22	Esth. 4-8	Ps. 108-114
I Kings 6-7	I Chr. 23-26	Esth. 9-10	Ps. 115-118
I Kings 8-9	I Chr. 27-28	Job 1-4	Ps. 119
I Kings 10-11	I Chr. 29	Job 5-9	Ps. 120-132
I Kings 12-13	II Chr. 1-3	Job 10-15	Ps. 133-141
I Kings 14-16	II Chr. 4-6	Job 16-20	Ps. 142-150
I Kings 17-18	II Chr. 7-10	Job 21-26	Ps. 1-5
I Kings 19-20	II Chr. 11-14	Job 27-31	Pro. 1-5
I Kings 21-22	II Chr. 15-18	Job 32-36	Pro. 6-10
II Kings 1-3	II Chr. 19-21	Job 37-39	Pro. 11-14
II Kings 4-5	II Chr. 22-24	Job 40-42	Pro. 15-19
II Kings 6-8	II Chr. 25-28	Ps. 1-10	Pro. 20-23
II Kings 9-10	II Chr. 29-30	Ps. 11-19	Pro. 24-27
II Kings 11-14	II Chr. 31-33	Ps. 20-27	Pro. 28-31
II Kings 15-16	II Chr. 34-35	Ps. 28-34	Ecc. 1-5
II Kings 17-18	II Chr. 36	Ps. 35-39	Ecc. 6-9
II Kings 19-21	Ezra 1-4	Ps. 40-46	Ecc. 10-12
II Kings 22-23	Ezra 5-7	Ps. 47-55	Song. 1-8
II Kings 24-25	Ezra 8-10	Ps. 56-63	Isa. 1-4
I Chr. 1-3	Neh. 1-3	Ps. 64-69	Isa. 5-8
I Chr. 4-5	Neh. 4-5	Ps. 70-76	Isa. 9-13
I Chr. 6-8	Neh. 6-9	Ps. 77-80	Isa. 14-18
I Chr. 9-11	Neh. 10-11	Ps. 81-88	Isa. 19-23
I Chr. 12-15	Neh. 12-13	Ps. 89-94	Isa. 24-28
I Chr. 16-18	Esth. 1-3	Ps. 95-103	Isa. 29-31

"But he answered and said, It is written, Man shall not live by bread alone, but by every word that proceedeth out of the mouth of God."

Matthew 4:4

YEAR BIBLE READING PLAN

Each day read the chapters listed. After you read the
daily reading put a line through it.

Example: ~~Gen. 1-4~~

Isa. 32-35			Matt. 28
Isa. 36-39			Mark 1-3
Isa. 40-42	Lam. 1-2	Hos. 7-14	Mark 4-5
Isa. 43-46	Lam. 3-4	Joel 1-3	Mark 6-8
Isa. 47-50	Ezek. 1-3	Amos 1-5	Mark 9-10
Isa. 51-55	Ezek. 4-7	Amos 6-9	Mark 11-13
Isa. 56-60	Ezek. 8-11	Obad 1	Mark 14-15
Isa. 61-64	Ezek. 12-15	Jonah 1-4	Mark 16
Isa. 65-66	Ezek. 16-17	Mic. 1-7	Luke 1-2
Jer. 1-3	Ezek. 18-20	Nah. 1-3	Luke 3-5
Jer. 4-6	Ezek. 21-22	Hab. 1-3	Luke 6-7
Jer. 7-9	Ezek. 23-25	Zeph. 1-3	Luke 8
Jer. 10-12	Ezek. 26-28	Hag. 1-2	Luke 9-10
Jer. 13-15	Ezek. 29-31	Zach. 1-7	Luke 11-12
Jer. 16-19	Ezek. 32-34	Zach. 8-11	Luke 13-15
Jer. 20-23	Ezek. 35-37	Zach. 12-14	Luke 16-18
Jer. 24-26	Ezek. 38-39	Mal. 1-4	Luke 19-20
Jer. 27-29	Ezek. 40-42	Matt. 1-4	Luke 21-22
Jer. 30-31	Ezek. 43-45	Matt. 5-7	Luke 23-24
Jer. 32-34	Ezek. 46-47	Matt. 8-10	John 1-3
Jer. 35-36	Ezek. 48	Matt. 11-13	John 4-5
Jer. 37-40	Dan. 1-3	Matt. 14-15	John 6-7
Jer. 41-43	Dan. 4-5	Matt. 16-18	John 8-10
Jer. 44-47	Dan. 6-8	Matt. 19-21	John 11-12
Jer. 48-49	Dan. 9-10	Matt. 22-23	John 13-15
Jer. 50-51	Dan. 11-12	Matt. 24-25	John 16-18
Jer. 52	Hos. 1-6	Matt. 26-27	John 19-21

"For the word of God *is* quick, and powerful, and sharper than any twoedged sword, piercing even to the dividing asunder of soul and spirit, and of the joints and marrow, and *is* a discerner of the thoughts and intents of the heart."
Hebrews 4:12

YEAR BIBLE READING PLAN

Each day read the chapters listed. After you read the daily reading put a line through it.

Example: ~~Gen. 1-4~~

Acts. 1-3		
Acts. 4-6		
Acts. 7-8	Col. 1-4	
Acts. 9-10	I Thes. 1-5	
Acts. 11-13	II Thes. 1-3	
Acts. 14-15	I Tim. 1-6	
Acts. 16-18	II Tim. 1-4	
Acts. 19-20	Titus 1-3	
Acts. 21-23	Phil. 1	
Acts. 24-26	Heb. 1-6	
Acts. 27-28	Heb. 7-10	
Rom. 1-3	Heb. 11-13	
Rom. 4-7	James 1-5	
Rom. 8-10	I Pet. 1-5	
Rom. 11-15	II Pet. 1-3	
Rom. 16	I Jn. 1-5	
I Cor. 1-5	II Jn. 1	
I Cor. 6-9	III Jn. 1	
I Cor. 10-13	Jude 1	
I Cor. 14-16	Rev. 1-3	
II Cor. 1-5	Rev. 4-6	
II Cor. 6-10	Rev. 7-9	
II Cor. 11-13	Rev. 10-11	
Gal. 1-6	Rev. 12-13	
Eph. 1-4	Rev. 14-16	
Eph. 5-6	Rev. 17-18	
Phil. 1-4	Rev. 19-22	

I have read my Bible from cover to cover.

Date
accomplished_____

X _____

Signature above

MY MEMORY VERSES

MAKE A LIST OF VERSES YOU HAVE MEMORIZED.

The Wind That Runs

Jesus said in John 3:8, "The wind bloweth where it listeth, and thou hearest the sound thereof, but canst not tell whence it cometh, and whither it goeth: so is every one that is born of the Spirit."

I went for a run the other day, and as I ran, some things came to me.

I started the race just as everyone else had. It was a beautiful day, the sun was at my back, and it just felt like a wonderful day. As I ran, the wind was against me, but the road was downhill.

As I ran, I felt comfort in knowing that others had and were traveling on the same road that I was. Some I had great respect for, they were out in front of me. Others I had contempt for, they were lagging way behind.

But I felt good as I ran. The only thing I didn't like was that the wind would push at me and slow me down. The road was wide and all downhill, but the wind would come at me and push. It seemed to want to push me in the opposite direction.

There were also occasions when I would pass a runner going the opposite direction, and we both thought the other strange. On one occasion, a man, running in the opposite direction, stopped me and told me that I was going the wrong way and that at the end would be destruction. I assured him that everyone was going this way and that he was odd to run the opposite of all mankind. I thought how silly he was to believe himself to be right and believe everyone else wrong. I continued on. After all, I did have moments of wonder, but I was enjoying the run.

I came to a stop sign as I ran. I paused for a moment and looked ahead. I saw others continuing on. So I continued. This occured twice more, and each time I looked ahead and pressed on. On the third occasion that I came to a stop sign, I tripped and fell. I had fallen before, but I never even gave it a second thought. I would just jump up, dust off, and run on. However, this time was different. I fell harder.

As I began to get up, I was on all fours and noticed a puddle of water below my face. I looked right at it and was truly bothered by what I saw! I saw my reflection... and as I paused, the wind that had been in my face suddenly seemed to open my eyes. I had had a picture of myself that was false. However, when I looked back into the puddle, I saw the devil in my eyes. I had been running for him: he was my master. As I looked ahead, I saw those who were running ahead. They continued even where there was no road. I watched those who had gone before me, those who I had admired who were ahead of me in the race. They had ran right past this final stop sign to where the road was no longer smooth and at the end was a cliff and at the bottom, a great lake of Fire.

So I turned, right then and there, and started to run in the opposite direction. As I ran, I noticed the road rise up to meet me in opposition. The road was all uphill, and those that had been running at my side were now running against me. But though the road opposed me, and though others ran in opposition to me, the same wind that had opposed me before now was in front of me, beside me, and behind me. That same wind was pushing me, calling me, and lifting me as I ran. I also realized that I was not alone in struggling against the current that came at me; there were others too! And how we wished we could open the eyes of even more so they would turn to the truth and run toward the sun (Jesus Christ), to follow in His steps.

You see, we all started the race at the same point. The first man who started the race ran in the wrong direction. His name was Adam, and everyone else has followed him ever since. All but one. One man came and started in the right direction.

The wind that was opposing me from the start was the Holy Spirit, and the sun that was at my back was the Son of God. God created the world and all that is. I had been running from Him my entire life; the farther I would run, the colder I became. I always had seen a few running opposite of the majority and thought them to be fools returning to the starting line. I never understood why anyone would want to go backward in a race not knowing that I and everyone but one, Jesus Christ, had started in the wrong direction. Those who were running back were not fools after all, but had realized the truth!

God had opened my eyes and had given me godly sorrow that lead to repentance, a complete 180 degree turn in the race. No longer did I want to run away from the warmth of the sun (Jesus Christ); no longer did I want to run in opposition to the wind (the Holy Spirit) and completely ignore the wonderful creation that God had made to show me the truth. I now was enlightened to know the way, the truth, and the life: Jesus Christ! This gave me great joy, even to run uphill against the current of the world, and to compel them that ran in the opposite direction to join me. For whether we run toward the sun or away from the sun, our race will be short in the span of eternity.

Those who run toward the sun (the Son of God, Jesus Christ) run to obtain eternal life through Jesus Christ , and they will spend eternity in Heaven praising Him for the perfect race that He ran. For we could not run that race, but were pleased to follow Him. We give up the short pleasures of this life, for the eternal pleasure of an eternity with God! Those who run away from the sun (the Son of God, Jesus Christ) run to obtain a corruptible crown that will surely rust and fade away. They run for the present physical wealth that will not last. No matter how hard they run, no matter how fast they go, no matter how well they seem to do, the truth remains that it is all for naught in the wrong direction. After their race here on earth, they will awake to eternal death and suffering in the flames of hell for all eternity. They sought their pleasure in this short life only to forfeit the pleasures in the next! So they had pleasure in the physical life in trade for eternal separation from God (all goodness comes from God). Hell is the final destination for those who run with the world.

Oh sinner, wake up! You are running with your back to the sun (Jesus Christ), the mercy of God. The wind (Holy Spirit) is blowing against you to awaken you out of your blindness! Many have gone before you to destruction and eternal ruin, don't follow them just because they are the majority! The Truth is Jesus! Those who follow Him, follow Life, those who oppose Him follow death!

Psa 19:5 Which *is* as a bridegroom coming out of his chamber, *and* rejoiceth as a strong man to run a race.

1Co 9:24 Know ye not that they which run in a race run all, but one receiveth the prize? So run, that ye may obtain.

Heb 12:1-2 Wherefore seeing we also are compassed about with so great a cloud of witnesses, let us lay aside every weight, and the sin which doth so easily beset *us,* and let us run with patience the race that is set before us, Looking unto Jesus the author and finisher of *our* faith; who for the joy that was set before him endured the cross, despising the shame, and is set down at the right hand of the throne of God.

References:

Scripture: King James Bible

Cover Design: SelfPubBookCovers.com/RLSather

Contact:

Nathan M. Noyes

nathannoyes@yahoo.com

Made in the USA
Coppell, TX
28 December 2019